HORSES

Illustrated by Henri Galeron
Produced by Gallimard Jeunesse
and Henri Galeron

A FIRST DISCOVERY B

SCHOLASTIC INC.
New York   Toronto   London   Auckland   Sydney

There are all kinds of horses,
small horses like this
Dartmoor pony...

...and big ones like the
Selle Francais or
Camargue, the "white
horse of the sea."

Shetland
pony

A horse has a short coat, a mane, a forelock
of hair between its ears, and a long tail.
Different breeds have different color coats.

the croup

tail

Yellow Dun

Bay

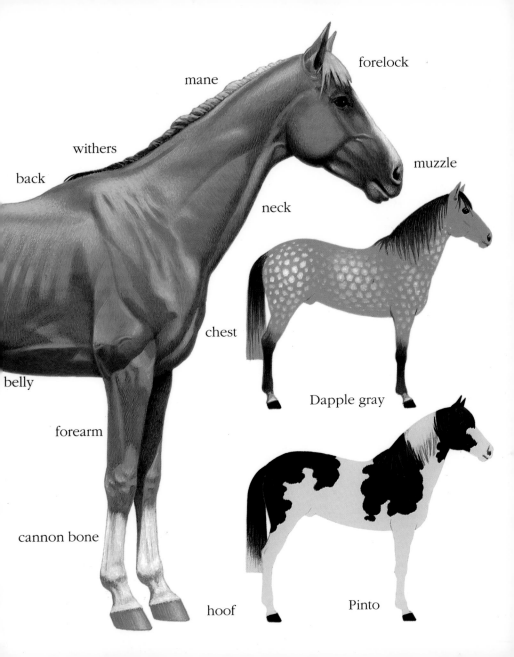

mane

forelock

withers

back

muzzle

neck

chest

belly

Dapple gray

forearm

cannon bone

hoof

Pinto

Here are different types of horses
from the largest horse to the smallest pony:

Shire

Percheron

Pinto

Appaloosa

Camargue/
"White horse
of the Sea"

Thoroughbred

Selle Francais

Przewalski's horse
or Asian wild horse

Shetland

Falabella

The pregnant mother or mare waits eleven months before giving birth.

Another horse often keeps her company.

When the baby horse or foal is born, its mother licks it clean and dry. This helps the foal to learn its mother's scent and feel warm and safe.

Most wild horses are born in the springtime.
When winter comes, they will be strong.

From its earliest days, the foal gambols after
its mother. For five or six months, they will
stay together.

Within an hour or two
after birth, the foal gets
on its feet to drink its
mother's milk.

A horse can sleep in several positions.

It can sleep while
standing up.

It sleeps more soundly
while lying down,

but horses never sleep
for long. They're ready
to run at the slightest
sign of danger.

hay

wheat
straw
for
bedding

alfalfa

Just like you,
the horse likes to eat
many different kinds
of food.

In order not
to drop any food,
this horse eats
out of a sack.

It replaces the salt
it loses by licking
a salt block.

oats

carrots

grain

You can tell a horse's age by the condition of its teeth. A horse's teeth never stop growing and have to be filed down.

A horse can drink up to ten gallons of water in a single day!

The farrier nails horseshoes to the horses' hooves. This protects them.

The stablehand uses a sponge, a body brush, and a mane comb
to groom the horse and keep its skin clean and healthy.

The blacksmith
shapes the metal into
a horseshoe when
it is softened by the heat.

English saddle   sidesaddle

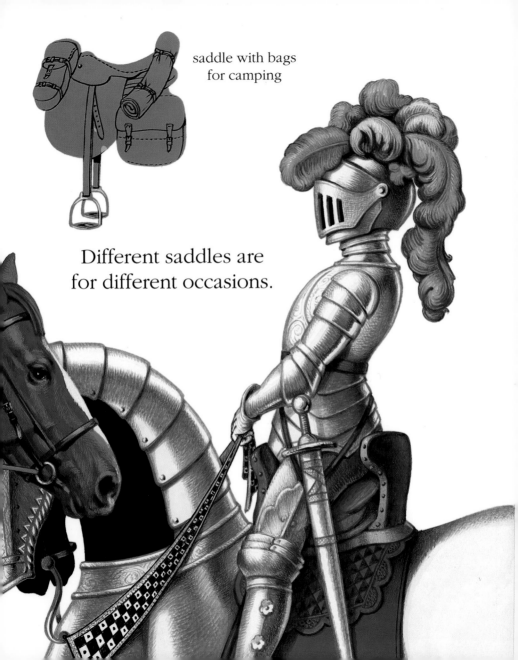

saddle with bags
for camping

Different saddles are
for different occasions.

A horse is very powerful
and jumps easily
over fences.

It moves slowly when at a walk, then moves faster when trotting,
increases speed in a canter...

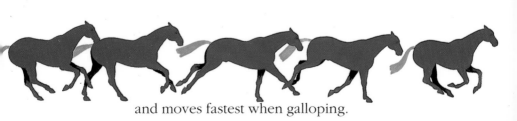

and moves fastest when galloping.

As part of a team of horses, it can pull a carriage...

Ever since people have tamed horses for work in the fields,

The horse sometimes performs in a circus or a rodeo show.

a sulky...

or even a wagon.

horses have
helped people to
do their work.

What do these animals have in common?

tapir

rhino

donkey

zebra

They all have hooves!

donkey
of Poitou

wild donkey
of Africa

domestic donkey

Parents Magazine
"Best Books" Award

**Parenting Magazine*
Reading Magic Award

****Oppenheim Toy Portfolio*
Gold Seal Award

Library of Congress Cataloging-in-Publication Data available.

Originally published in France under the title *Le Cheval* by Editions Gallimard Jeunesse.

ISBN 0-590-96216-7

Copyright © 1991 by Editions Gallimard Jeunesse.
This edition English translation by Heather Miller.
This edition American text by Wendy Barish.
This edition Expert Reader: Liz Hoskinson, Director of Corporate Communications,
American Horse Shows Association, Inc.
All rights reserved. First published in the U.S.A. in 1997 by Scholastic Inc., by arrangement with Editions Gallimard Jeunesse.

SCHOLASTIC and the SCHOLASTIC logo are registered trademarks of Scholastic Inc.

12 11 10 9 8 7 6 5 4 3 2 1   7 8 9/9 0 1 2/0

Printed in Italy by Editoriale Libraria

First Scholastic printing, August 1997